I HAVE NO NAME

THREADS

L'CHAIM

a life in poetry

Marie Davis Cameron

Mt Nittany Press
Lemont | Berlin

DEDICATION

Having lived a good long life, I am now a great-grandmother with extended family. I dedicate this book to the newest generation:

Logan Blue Riney
Sloane Violet Riney
Madison Ann Harrell
Caden Glen Harrell
Jai-Lynn Ashley Davenport
Liliana Shae Fox-Stowe

L'Chaim! My Darlings.

M.D.C.

"And ships that sail will return to port."

© 2022 Marie Davis Cameron
Cover design by David Corona
Printed in the United States of America

All rights reserved. This publication is protected by Copyright, and permission should be obtained from the publisher prior to any prohibited reproduction, storage in a retrieval system, or transmission in any form or by any means, electronic, mechanical, photocopying, recording, or likewise.

Published by Eifrig Publishing,
PO Box 66, Lemont, PA 16851.
Knobelsdorffstr. 44, 14059 Berlin, Germany

For information regarding permission, write to:
Rights and Permissions Department,
Eifrig Publishing,
PO Box 66, Lemont, PA 16851, USA
permissions@eifrigpublishing.com, 814.954.9445

Library of Congress Cataloging-in-Publication Data

Cameron, Marie Davis., 1936-
    I Have No Name ~Threads ~ L'Chaim: a life in poetry / Marie Davis Cameron

Under the name Maria Landowska, *I Have No Name* was originally published in 1984 by Marymack Publishing and was considered for the Pulitzer Poetry Prize for that year. The author wishes to make clear that *I Have No Name* is not a personal family story. It is a compilation of many Holocaust stories told to her by survivors while in psychotherapy, which have been woven, along with her own memories of this time, into a more impactful epic poem.
Threads was originally published in 1985 by Nortex Press and was awarded the Eleventh Annual Nortex Award for poetry that year.
L'Chaim (To Life) is a new publication and the author's definitive work, sharing the shaping influences decade by decade until the reader realizes Cameron's "family" now encircles all segments of society and reaches out to infinity.

  p.   cm.

Paperback: ISBN 978-1-63233-335-3
Hardcover: ISBN 978-1-63233-336-0

    1. Poetry, 2. Jewish History 3. Holocaust
I. Cameron, Marie Davis II. Title.

26 25 24 23 2022
5 4 3 2 1

Printed on acid-free paper. ∞

*". . . And the fire
and the rose are one."*
T. S. Eliot

I HAVE NO NAME
(1984)

In the beginning –
Each day was like a candle newly lit
Endowing everything around it
With a soft, glowing beauty
For the memory's eye to see.
Candles on the white, white tablecloth,
The golden loaves, the crimson wine,
                And the five of us.

And then –
The Star of David worn over the heart,
Plucked from the heavens to stand apart.
Papa said, "Wear it and be proud."
We stood in anguish, unbowed.
There were hobnailed boots that stopped at our door;
Mama kissed him and called him Jacob,
                And then there were four.

We ran –
As the young follow the flag of the doe,
Averting our eyes from the scarlet snow.
But Abe was young and full of fight,
One slight man against such might.
We hungered but we were free,
He starved for music, books, so much more,
                Until we were three.

We hid –
But where can you hide from the spitting fire;
Where from the fearful vision of barbed wire
When cities have a million eyes
With no one to believe your lies.
We were glad when death came that no one knew
Our sweet Mama had reached such depths,
      But then we were two.

And finally –
I stood encompassed by a wall of stone.
The world was at peace but I was alone.
Questing voices asked me my name.
The answer was always the same:
There was Jacob and Abe (these things I knew),
Mama and sister – but I have no name –
      Just call me a Jew.

This is Maria's story,
my story;
the story of a small family,
a psalm of decreasing numbers.
It is not a history,
not a well known
tale of six million Jews.
I never knew six million Jews.
I knew five loving people;
We lived in a house on
Lindenstrasse,
lived together, close together
with love and words and music.
We each died alone –
Not in our own time,
But what is death?
And what is time?

*My memories are a prism
dangling in sunlight;
I turn the prism,
it sparkles blue.
I turn it again,
it gleams red.
Brief poignant pictures
rise to the foreground –
Abe sketching flowers in the garden,
Papa's hands caressing the ivories
of the piano:
Margot running,
tripping down the
crimson carpeted staircase;
And my mother's eyes –
Maggie's eyes –
looking, soft and loving,
gazing across the candles,
melting into Papa's eyes.
Those early memories are warm;
They are sunlit memories,
those memories before the lights went out
in the house on Lindenstrasse.
The prism gleams,
It dangles in the sunlight and gleams –
dangles and gleams.*

Papa-

*He strides across my childhood
shaking a finger at Plato,
haranguing him,
"Your Republic is inherently
unrealistic," he protests.
To Pliny, and Cicero,
To Pericles and Socrates,
he says,
"Meet Maria. You are welcome
in her mind's house."
And they entered.
And there they abode
in my winter,
sharing the cold of
my camp years.
Papa loved with music
and with words,
and the philosophers –
all the ancient ones –
kept him good company.*

No snowy white doves on the altar,
no new-born lambs for the sacrifice.
The Nazis replaced them.
They did better.
They offered up their best:
Their finest artists,
Their most erudite philosophers.
   O Papa,
   You were always in such good company.

*****

Papa strung the violin,
All the while listening to me,
Perched on worktable, legs swinging free.

Placing cheek against the wood
And drawing bow across the string,
He heard his two instruments sing.

Holding knife in his square hand,
He would cut and shave the "F" hole
The way his questions shaped my soul.

Papa played the violin.
Creating its balance and tone,
Papa taught me to stand alone.

*Papa had no
empty-handed answers
for children;
He was a method-father;
A good question deserved
a good question response;
A non-good question
deserved silence.
He was friendly with few absolutes,
finding his comfort
in the mathematical
equations of music,
And in the constantly
rotating wheel of
civilizations –
"The curve of history,"
he called it.*

*****

*I course in a straight line through history
While civilizations curve around me.
I watch the Roman peak fall away
To the Germanic rise of today,
Knowing we are as barbaric as they.*

*Papa's vocation was
the interpretation
of music.
His avocation,
the music of
philosophers;
his absolute truth was
discipline.*

*He constantly tested
his own depths,
an absent-minded ruler
in our household
until the toast of
occasions.
Then the fire of belief
flared from the wine goblet
to envelope his lean frame.
"To us," he would say,
"To the family,
To our music,
To our discipline;
We may leave the family,
Lose our music,
And we will never
Lose our discipline."
"The discipline" meant
as a family,
we sweat together.
At dawn,
chromatic scales
bombarded the house
until I slid off
the wet piano bench.
Papa was there,
Mine in the early hours.*

*Abraham was in his
alone time,
taunted by mellow,
cello tones –
to excel,
to discipline,
to excel.
Margot had Maggie
and they stretched
and pleyeed at
the ballet barre
until we all shared
the same damp state
together.*

Mama –

> *Papa called her*
> *"the beautiful barbarian"*
> *and she was.*
> *Her strength was her pride*
> *like the rock of her*
> *Scottish hills;*
> *Her hair was the kiss*
> *of golden-glow sunset.*
> *One eye was blue,*
> *the other brown;*
> *Scots made the hex sign*
> *when she passed.*
> *Love made Maggie blind*
> *to the other sight.*

*Memory parts the curtain of years –
the indifferent baton swings right,
it swings left;
The flesh is torn from the bone
and she strides quickly away,
tangled mass of sunrays
bouncing on her back.
I cry, "Mama, look back at me."
Her pace quickens.
She runs to death,
to her love,
to Jacob,
already waiting on
the other side.*

*The childish mind
is incapable of
comprehending
the myriad mysteries
of mature loving.
It made no sense to me.
Book-possessing,
idea-cherishing
Papa,
adored physical
Maggie
who never read
and rarely reasoned.
Maggie,
who just was:
wild, willful, devoted
to the dance.*

*Maggie's energy went
into the perfection
of her body;
She was the ultimate pirouette;
She was prima,
In ballet,
In Papa's heart.
All introspective
patience she had
was his.
Margot did not need it,
Abe did not want it.
Only Maria,
enmeshed in
mental meanderings
yearned
for mind contact
with Maggie.
Maria called the lack,
"mother love."*

*It was not.
Maggie's motherhood
was not to be
expressed in words.
Papa walked
a road of words.
Maggie's way was
will and strength.
Two days of night
incarcerated within
cramped,
suffocating,
wood and steel,
with time
lost in a space
of fresh air
and forgotten stars.
Two days of night
entombed with
moaning humanity.
In my remembering now
there is only the
smell of Maggie's flesh,
the bonding of her arms
with our twin bodies.*

*She was Athena
straining to hold
upright
her fragile world.
Others clutched
broken treasures
of earthly value;
Maggie protected
her posterity,
protected
the gems in
her crown.*

*(I live, Mama.
And sharing
my living space
is a wild and
willful child of
prideful strength.
She has no patience
with my prodding mind
and would rather
walk en pointe.
You live, Mama.)*

Abraham –

> *My older brother,*
> *You are a*
> *shadow on*
> *memory's wall.*
> *You are a*
> *feeling of*
> *solicitude,*
> *lines on a*
> *sketch pad,*
> *cello strains,*
> *a playful hand*
> *ruffling my hair.*
> *You are a love feeling.*

*The lights went out
and Abraham
backed into a black hole.
Did he meet
demons or angels there?
God knows,
Abraham knows;
No one else.*

Abraham died
And Avram was born;
Abraham lost his hand
and his music;
Avram found his God;
Abraham lost his homeland,
Avram found Israel.
Abraham left no children;
Avram's little ones wrote,
"Sister of Avram,
at this Kibbutz are many,
many children of your
brother's mind."

*War is hell and war is hate
and intrinsic man remains.
He becomes more of himself,
more of what he was in the first place.
Three decades descended
screening Abe from
my reality
and a gentle rabbi
dies.
My dead brother
is found;
My dead brother
is dead;
My legacy:
a yellowed photograph
of a stoop-shouldered man
surrounded by children
gazing up at him.
This looks like Papa.
Where is Abraham, Lord?
This is not enough!
"This was enough for Abraham,"
replies God.*

Margot –
> *My twin,*
> *I am sad.*
> *Your laughter bubbled,*
> *bursting from my*
> *childhood's spring.*
> *You vibrated in our space,*
> *you revelled in our lives.*
> *Now you remain transfixed,*
> *frozen forever*
> *on the barbed wire*
> *of our last years.*
> *It should not be.*
> *And it is.*
> *"Maria, look at all the edelweiss."*
> *That is what you said*
> *when the Angel of Death*
> *came our way.*

*What did Margot see
when the dark-hooded
stranger
came our way?*

*Edelweiss.
Intrepid white flower
hidden high in mountain crevice.
Plucked by the agile and strong.
Delicate white blossom
surviving in cold.
Torn out to prove victory
over height.*

*Edelweiss.
Pluck it.
Tear it out by the roots.
It will become dried dust;
Brown petals and browner leaves
filtering through the fingers
of the victors.
Margot was
Edelweiss.*

*Seeking my reflection
in the glass,
I see a distorted
Margot.
A rifle blow
broke my jaw,
sights tore my face.
I still see her
shining
in my eyes.
L'enfant tristesse et
L'enfant heurheuse,
we two.
I always knew living
was a serious,
painful process.
For Margot,
Living was joy,
and she was joy,
and joy ran
on winged feet.
When living ceased
to be joy,
Margot left.*

*She walks in the front row
Of the photograph,
Dark eyes faintly aglow,
lips hinting a laugh;
lips learning to supplicate.
(Dear God, do not let me hate.)*

*She walks in the front row
Of a long, long line,
Gleaning from the ghetto,
See David's star shine!
I can taste each tender tear.
(Dear God, do not let me fear.)*

*She walks in the front row
Clutching Mother's hand,
Trusting Mother to know;
Can she understand
The man-beasts who thwart her fate?
(Dear God, do not let me hate.)*

*She walks in the front row
Of my waking dream.
She should stay and I go;
I scream her last scream.
What could she contaminate?
(Dear God, do not let me hate.)*

*She walks in the front line
Of humanity;
Tasting vinegar wine
Of the Trinity.
Where did Jesus walk that day?
(Dear God, help me find my way.)*

*Margot left.
I was alone
and in pain.*

*Pain lives on
Loneliness Island.
I tried hating
the fortunate
dead ones.
Still,
life was honey
and I savored
the sweet taste.
I made a decision
to live another day,
and then another,
and another.
It became a habit.
All because of Euripides.
Euripides threw mud
into a fountain.
The gushing waters
washed the mud away.
Then Euripides said to me,
"Keep your soul's spring pure
and nothing, nothing
will ever dirty you."*

How dark the moon that night he came to me
Punishing my lack of humility;
He plunged and pierced me with his sword again,
Reopened my wound, renewed my pain.

Renewed our war within the greater war,
Claiming conquest he had not made before,
But I parted spirit from this,
This act of venom, this viper's kiss.

How wild the wind that night he came to me,
How easily my mind was wafted free;
Though my body lay imprisoned still,
My soul soared above his devil's will.

"You lost on the bed of battle," he said,
And he caressed my body as I bled.
"You will break and some day they will tell
How I rode you to the gates of hell."

And ride me to the gates of hell, he did,
But he rode through and I remained and lived.
He went to ashes, to dust without love,
While I became the steel mourning dove.

*The self-inflicting
sword of guilt
grew heavier
and more deadly
as I hid
from the minor
pogrom within
the major
genocide.
All of me
cried
for mercy.
But I wielded the sword
and there
was no mercy
in me
for me.
There was only
food gulped
unshared,
shoes stolen
from the dead,
and knowledge
that when
I refused to die,
someone else did.*

Dark eyes,
Glowing coals,
The depths of sunflowers;
And where is the sun?
In my hand –
A carrot.
Remnant from a lost garden,
Soil ashed with remains
of the gardener?
Sharp eyes turned to
dark eyes pleading
beyond my wire.
As I hid to eat
the carrot
I tried not to ask
myself:
Would he live?
Did he care to live?
In some other life
would he have stepped
on the cup
beneath my canopy?

*I heard the
Shema
one day.
A man was
dying.
Hear, O Israel.
Warm tears seeped
from eyes
that wondered
what they were.
And I met
a more
intimate hunger –
a hunger to touch
the face of
my Creator.
Searching within,
I found Him there.
And then,
I had no name.*

I was Esther in the palace;
She was my handmaiden;
She lived with a raping reality
and angered herself with
my imagination;
And still; she humored
my childish escapes,
serving me well –
Tina.
Daughter of a daughter
of a gypsy –
Beautiful bones found
on wall tracings
of Egyptian tombs;
Tina,
With a frescoed heart
that I chipped away on
while she stormed
my citadel of dreams.
There never was a winner.
She died not knowing
I knew
what she knew.

*There had to be someone
left to
sit shiva,
lean close to the earth
to mourn;
There had to be someone
left to
say kaddish,
memorial prayers
to adorn.
I asked
God
how to survive
and heard,
"keep on breathing."
So I did.
It was not living;
It was surviving.
I nurtured myself.
Rilke and Milton
met one another
in my mind
until I noticed
the strait was narrow.
My Creator swam
with me from
Loneliness Island
to the Continent of Humanity.*

The Continent of Humanity:
I have walked
its misty shore
of dreams,
Climbed its heights
of hope,
Foraged its forests.
There I learned
the ecstasy
of the touching.
I have seen my pain
in another's eyes,
felt my pain intensified –
That is the touching.
There is the moment
of sighing,
The moment of
withheld tears,
The desertion of self,
The reaching across
the void of night;
The hand held,
The unspoken word.
I and thou
become one
in The Touching.

*They needed bread
and medicine.
Maria, the child,
gave flowers –
Words blooming
again in my mind:
Byron, Keats, Shelley;
A flow of words
they did not understand.
I was a river
of rhyme
and many drowned.
It was a strange
way to die.
Polish and German Jews
listening
to English poets.
As good a way as any,
I guess;
It was all
I had
to give.*

*I saw an elegant lady die
and she did it elegantly
filling her dying with a leaf –
just one leaf
outside the window.*

*I saw an old woman share her bread.
I ate that bread.
Three generations had come
from her body.
They were all dead.
So she nurtured me;
She took bread from her body
until she was no more.*

*The time came when
there was nothing left;
I was thirteen;
There was nothing –
nothing left of me –*

Nothing –

*Only Jacob's words and music,
Maggie's will and strength,
Margot's laughter,
And Abraham's love.*

I hear Your Feet upon the mountaintop
I see Your Shadow on the plain,
I call and beg for You to pause or stop
That I may know Your love again;

I am the fawn beside the water
I am the lamb they could not slaughter.
I am the tigress with her kitten
I am the psalms that must be written
I am the oak, I am the willow
I am the head without a pillow;

I am part of every Jew who trod
Through the Kamps of Hell to meet his God.

After

Never Again!
Ripped bodies no longer fell;
The war of the age
culminated in
a roar of rage
as we ascended from Hell.

Never Again!
Blind eyes were forced to see
the dead bones of
Sarahs and Abrahams,
the living bones of me.

Never Again!
(British slammed
Palistinian gates;
Cypress transformed
wood to wire.)
Jewish voices
choked with fervor,
smoked with fire.

Never again
to experience
cruel Gentile steel,
crueler Gentile pain.

*I lay interred
and whimpering
as they tore apart
the floor boards
over my coffin.
Liberators
splintered
hands and nails
to lift me
from the grave.*

*I was a basket of eggs,
just as precious,
and tenderly passed,
until I came to rest
in strong arms
looking into a
familiar,
unfamiliar face.*

How strange –
Jewish eyes beneath
a military helmet,
Jewish head crowning
a uniform.
He racked himself
with my bones
until he slid
to the ground
outside B-1-A
compound.
There,
holding me close
while rocking in
the age-old way,
I heard a
new-age Jew pray –

    And I entered my After.

*Our liberators
wished to wash
us with the
water of nobility.
A difficult task.
We were not noble.
We were
tubercular and ugly.
We were
whining silence.*

*We were not noble.
We were the
fortunate
left to question
Luck's lot.
Our liberators
forgot
Lucifer was beautiful,
(Bright star of the morning);
We were simply
human.*

*Liberate me!
Can you free me
of dread decisions
made?
Of variegated visions
of inner self?
Of days of death
and nights of stealth,
and grinding gut
that chews on
sudden loud word,
sudden dropped spoon?
Can you free me of
my monsoon
of emotions
and endless
illuminous
oceans of now?*

*Draw a diagram
of who I am
as I try to
remember
my name
and blow on
the ember
of familial loss.*

*Try to sustain
my fragile frame
as I guard the
flickering
Shabbat flame
within.*

See six screams,
Hear my dreams,
Feel an orangy hue,
I'm me – ME – not you.

White witchcraft,
Lost life raft,
I need a good view
Of myself – not you.

My God's near,
Hold Him here,
My devil is too,
I'm me – ME – not you.

See six screams,
Hear my dreams,
Secure my mind-line;
Christ, where are MY swine?

*After
was a pink-icinged
confection
too rich for
consuming.*

*Once,
in the memory-house
on Lindenstrasse,
I rested my chin
on Cook's table
to watch her
build it.
Now I was expected
to devour it.*

*I spent days
vomitting food.
I spent years
vomitting memories.*

*Memory
clings to the
kinesthetic.
A draft across
bare shoulders.
The place –
a fine restaurant.
The occasion –
Congenial dinner.*

*The place?
No –
Hell!
The occasion –
Hanging by wrists,
tearing shoulders,
the itch of
blood trickling.
(Golda died that day.)*

*A draft across
bare shoulders,
a pause in dinner,
momentary paralysis;
I rub scarred wrists,
scratch a memory,
and say,
"Pass the salt, please."*

*Memory has a potent picture
power superimposed on
bas relief
in a museum...
The imaginative child,
Maria,
rises from within
to claim
Tina,
her dead friend.*

*Memory is in the crunch
of a carrot.
Jaw-movement halts,
stomach growls
while tongue
experiences
bitter-sweet taste
of another time
and the inner eye
memorializes
pleading
dark eyes.*

*Remembrance is in
fragrance of flowers
floating through
open window,
drifting through
my dreams of the
rainbow-yearning child,
finger-writing
in the dust.*

I am a drained-grey rainbow;
The flowers have all disappeared
And I do not know where they went;
I remember –
They were soft to touch
And full of color and sweet scent;
I know I could stand this cruel rain
If, before I die,
I could just see flowers again.

*I tried to turn
the collar of Time
and I could not
mend it.
The Dresden
ballerina
was broken.
My Rosenthal
teacup childhood
was shattered.*

*I could not penetrate the
stalactites and
stalagmites formed
in the frost of
my camp years.
Silent sentinels,
they stood,
in the between
of my past.
There was only
one turning
for me –
the trudge
toward
tomorrow.*

Father –
*   I was alone*
*   and every word*
*   was a sentry*
*   with outthrust bayonet.*
*   I lived in a void,*
*   a dark pit*
*   without a floor,*
*   and I feared*
*   that loathesome*
*   part of me*
*   that must lead*
*   to Hades' door.*

*I was alone
and he came
out of the crowd
and held out
his hand to me.*

*I took his hand
and we walked
together into
a rolling land
of soft
Gaelic voices.*

*We watched a wave
leaping against a rock,
reaching to pluck
a diamond
from the sky;*

*(And he told me
my mother
would never die
as long as I
held her within.)*

*We rode our
riverway on
varnished wood,
and planted trees,
examined a leaf
and all its
intricacies;*

*(And I learned
a man could be
totally good.)*

*He taught me
to search autumn
sky for lights
that trace the path
to heaven.
He made me believe
it was
September's gown
that touched
maples and alders
to their glory.
And that she
waited just
beyond the hills
for her lover,
the stronger October,
to join her.*

*He said that
November,
first of
winter's children
would weave
a spread
of delicate snowflakes
and frozen dewdrops
for their bed.*

*(He asked me to
call him Father
"for I am not
your Papa
and never could be.")*

*I called him Father
and also,
God's mercy,
for that great oak
of a Scot
breathed new
life into me.*

*To begin again
is pain.*

*Winding roads through
dark woods
with only one light,
one clear light
to lead the way.*

*To begin again
is joy.*

*Breath-holding adventure;
New paths to explore.*

*Gone, monotonous,
rigidly structured days.
Gone, scare and hate
and not understanding.
Hello risk,
and loving and caring,
and still
not understanding.*

*So goes the search for self
on the way back.*

*I met five gurus
On Armageddon Road;
Broke their bread,
Shared my wine.
They departed thirsty
While I hungered.*

*The first teacher
Showed me acceptance –
He shared my weakness in his strength,
I shared his strength in my weakness –
I laughed at me and liked him.*

*The second guru
Gave me loving until
I enshrined part of him in part of me;
And when the DNA snowflake melted,
I learned my love is to release.*

*The third guru
Held a sword in his tongue
And he slashed at space until I thrust
Myself upon his cutting edge –
I learned for me pain is not noble.*

*The fourth guru
Held a mirror before me
And I hated him for my expectations,
And all my wasted wanderings:
And I met the fifth guru.*

*I met five gurus
On my millennium road;
I have vanquished all but one –
The one who knows.*

*****

*I am.
What else?
My apple may be a grape.
And so my love may be rape.
Myself.
All else could exist but me:
Mad, deaf, unable to see.
Not so.
I know
God is
I am.*

*My respect of self
has become crustacean.
It clings to my essence
as coral clings
to the reef;
I believe that respect
of self shares
beauty with the coral.
It also shares a
cutting edge
for those who
wish to change me.*

*For once,
there were five
in a house
on Lindenstrasse,
and now there
is one.*

*Once,
there was a child named
Maria
who died in the
Kamps of Hell.
And once,
I had no name.*

Where has all the pain gone?
Exorcised?
Cauterized?
Acts God would not rescind –
Torn away,
Borne away,
By the impartial wind.

Where has all the grief gone?
Prayers to spin
Held within?
No tears left now to fall –
Torn away,
Borne away,
Left at the wailing wall.

THREADS
(1985)

Table of Contents

At The Line Camp
In The Car
To Denver
To Los Angeles
At The Hospital

At the Line Camp

The girls and I were working
the crosscut saw
when Joe rode in.
The old sheltering oak
had come crashing,
reasonless,
in the night, and we
thirsted to thin
the branches of
nocturnal fright.

I was telling them not to push,
but pull,
enjoying the continuity
of saying what
Father had said to me.
We were full of
the together-laughter
that comforts mothers
and daughters after
their parting.

Joe's horse was scarred
with foam flecks and dust
so I knew he must
have been riding hard.

His eyes met mine,
then flitted down,
and away, and my heart began
its last crying,
even before I heard him say,
"Ma'am, it's your Daddy;
he's dying."

Shuddering winds
of change
blew across my plain
as I was buffeted
by a hurricane
of pain.

There was no time
to fill emptiness
with tears;
no time to lag.
We had not washed
and there was
such a lack
of clothes,
I could only pack
one small bag
to fling on
saddle horn.
I kissed the girls.
Later, later,
we would mourn.

I could feel
him calling
as I attacked the
raw-tongued road.
In Horse Canyon,
I vaguely recall
a black bull
bawling
on the hill,
his voice echoing
in the still
morning air.
I did not care.
I was propelled
into the future,
wondering how
I would suture
the wounds of now.

In the Car

I horse-rode ten line-camp miles
and car-drove another twenty,
counting word-beads, love, and smiles
strung on memories of plenty.
I made a stage of the car window,
sat back, and let the movie reel flow,
looking straight into a day in forty-five
when the me-child, barely alive,
war-ravished by bitterness and hate,
stood wanting at Humanity's gate,
with no one willing to turn the key
until that great oak of a man
smiled and said he wanted me.

He was a wandering man
of salt-sea and sky,
with oceans for thoughts
and fathomless words
a child could build on,
a child could live by.

The wise (who know all so well)
said I was regurgitated by Hell,
and that he should not be confused
into thinking he could
save a soul so abused.
He just said, "Time will tell."

He fed and cherished me and taught
what my hungry brain had thought
it would never chance to learn.

Then we worked, clearing the land,
until I was too bone-weary to stand,
and would drop into bed
too worn for crushing hates
that had to be self-fed.
They starved there, inside me,
and one day I awoke ... Free.

He took me to a misty island of
molded hills and rocky shore
and I talked of before
for the first time.

I remembered,
azure sky and emerald grass
and grinding pain,
pain that would not pass,
and a gentle man
delivering me.

Father shared my fantasy
of constant flowing light
on the sea of infinity.
I became possessed
by words again
that fell as acid drops
upon my brow,
rivalling tears of
incessant rain;
all the tears my memories
would allow.

Father shared my rainbow
of clear, shimmering thought,
clinging like the sand
wafted through Time's land.
I became obsessed
with life again,
aware of iridescent energy,
a promise-bright,
sun-stroked stained
glass pane,
as life's sweet elixirs
flowed on through me.

I remembered,
long-held splendor
on golden grass
and endless joy,
joy that did not pass,
with the mindful man
who rescued me.

We buttered our bread
with words that year,
sliding them
across the table
when we meal-sat;
there was no fat
in our close sharing;
just the lean
of mutual caring
deposited between.

O'Dell met me in town
with his small plane,
and I began
the counting again,
stringing my life-beads
on a weighty chain.

To Denver

As we winged
noon-sky,
I asked
how I would
say goodbye
to his razor-wit
challenging me,
and if it mattered
that I could
not fit
into his
woman-mold.
I would miss
his eagle-swoop
on my household.
And who was left
to battle me
on Right?
(I was always
Gray Reason,
while he was
Black and White.)

He called me
judgemental
and I retorted,
"I try to be perfect!"
He laughed, and said,
"Who ... You ... Red?"
We laughed
together
and I continued
to judge
the judgemental.

Roads bend,
trees bend,
children fall to
their knees
and bend,
lovers who want
to please,
they bend,
but we know,
my friend,
preachers never bend.

Roads run,
streams run,
children who scream
loud screams,
will run,
wild things
God esteems,
they run,
but when all
is done,
preachers do not run.

Life takes,
earth takes,
a child rises
In his mirth
and takes,
but faced with
high stakes,
every preacher breaks.

Metal-reflected flash
in the cockpit
precipitates scare
and the question
who will care
for my girls
if we are all gone.

I have an adrenalin
flashback of my own ...
Mary on the telephone:
"C. B.'s plane burned,
all dead."

The black sea came
crashing in on me,
and I scrubbed floors
and scrubbed floors
until I felt her presence.
I looked up and saw her ...
Clara Bess looking down,
laughing;
laughing at me
scrubbing floors.
I laughed too.

Gone raven peak
and tapered hand;
Gone her will
to understand.
"My days are coined,"
she said,
"And spend them I must."
She squandered time with love
before she went to dust.

I never understood
why C.B.
would not respond
to the world's
expectations.
God gives some the
grace to know they
have limited
trivia-time.

To Los Angeles

I leaned into the skyship,
closed my eyes,
and tried to iron
the wrinkles from
the fabric of my life,
and realized,
it was not
varicolored beads
I had been counting,
but vibrating threads;
threads woven into
the tapestry
of my existence.
Looking into the face
of my fierce-vaunted
independence,
I thought I detected
a farcical,
self-deluding pretense.

Blending regal
indigo and gold,
maroons and purple,
Maria wove a tapestry
of dreams and fixed
it on her castle wall.
Many gazed and later
would recall
its shifting, silken
shades of delight.
They would remember,
and wonder whither
went that tapestry
when Maria
joined the night.

Blending colors of
baked hill-grass
and red clay
with lambswool gray,
Anna wove for her son,
a saddle blanket
in the Navajo way.
And when the work
was done,
Joseph stroked it
with his hands,
his eyes seeking the
imperfection of
Anna's Spirit Line.
When he found it,
he smiled,
for his mother's soul
was not imprisoned
in the cloth's design.

Had I become
a facade of intent,
loss in the
firmament
of the written word?
Was my substance
locked in a
hospital bed
instead
of within
the woof and warp
of me?
Questions wrapped
in threads.

Donne-like,
I shook the
tapestry aloft
chasing, catching
the zigzag of
intricate design,
segregating
the will and thoughts
of others,
integrating
what was me and mine.

I recognized
White threads
of Mary,
black hair auraed
in silvern glow.
With gift of artist's eye,
she had taught me how to see.
Now, looking at grass,
grass is not green.
She took the nails
of my lost years
and drove them
into her body.
Somehow, she survived.
She became a
different Mary
and she still loved me.

There is a
polished pebble
in the pocket
of my mind,
and I find
it is a
witty-bright
word written
by you.

There is a
palette-perfect
painting canvassed
on my eye,
and I sigh
to think of
those three
torn treees
you drew
for me.

There is a
silvery-still
and silent place
in my soul;
I am whole
with the
light-lovely
lady who
dwells in me.

Green threads
spoke of Allen
who said there
was a pseudo-
humility in
kneeling,
when we talked
of God;
Allen, who
scotched feeling,
but I saw him
kneel to plant
a tree.
He taught me
I could love
without being
loved in return.

He said he was
no phantom
in my dreams,
no ghost
in my bed.
I thought,
he is he,
and became aware
of my reality;

He was greens growing,
a nurturing of life,
energy flowing.

He was need to care,
and not in overt ways
that choke and ensnare.
He was silent space,
absorbing all the pain,
ignoring the race.
I wanted to be
of that self-same pattern,
but then, I was me.

Lane's color
was loyal blue,
like his eyes.
I loved Lane once.
I remembered
in that space
of then:
his subtle humor
his listening quietude.

I was sand,
he was water;
he was water,
I was sand;
I was love left,
he was silence
I did not
understand.

I sifted under
the river,
while he flowed
over me,
and away,
and away.
We never met
to mix and mold
our clay.
Sand needs
water
to be shaped
and fulfilled;
water needs sand
to be purified
and distilled.

I left sensuous,
midnight-blue velvet,
touched the
saffron raw-silk
of sisterhood,
and sang an ode
to Eurasiana.

Saffron yellow,
soft and mellow,
is the glowing,
and the growing,
in the open-
ended place
of my lovingly
shared space
with Elsie-Mio.

Sweet melody,
and harmony,
touch the
bright flowers
of our late hours,
when compass points
do submit
to conversation
and wit
with Elsie-Mio.

We are blending;
I am mending
my illusion
of seclusion.
As sand falls
through the sifter,
I know I do
not differ
with Elsie-Mio.

I held earth-colors
of my chosen
younger sister who
once needed me,
and in exchange,
gave me
the gift of
my lost youth ...
Shara, my token Druid.

No one knows you
as I do, Shara,
for caring finds
a chink in armor,
penetrating the
outward charmer.

You are wispy-blue mist
with nothing to resist;
You are salty tears
sighing, sighing,
and dreams I can hear
crying, crying . . .

You are earthen hues
and golden green,
and tomorrows
of a silver sheen,
and a spirit
that is spirit-clean.
The earth knows you
as I do, Shara.

With an ache of awe
I caressed and traced
threads until I saw
that running
through them all,
from my Spring-green
to russet-Fall,
was a rope of
paternal gold
my two fathers
had mined.
What day had they
become combined
within me?

What could be
the meaning
of these two
careening
in the nucleus of me?

One plus one, equals two,
(mathematically uncompared).
Algebraically,
plus blood and bone, plus
minus blood and bone
could equalize,
becoming one squared,
through common-love shared.

I was touched by
the fluttering thrush
of understanding
as my carrier-condor
prepared for landing.

Looking out at
sea of stars and
mirror-like lights,
I saw again,
the lilies of my youth.

When I was young
I travelled
a blue-green road
on varnished wood
with watery pebbles
slapping every side;
I skimmed and glided
where I went,
leaving a trail
the river was
swift to hide.
I pleased myself
with Freedom,
and teased myself
with Truth,

as I rode the river
in search of
water lilies
in my youth.

I kept the secret
of Red Archie's
hidden still,
and the poetic why
of the lone loon's
haunting cry.
Only I could
discern the tree
that marked the grave
of Indian lover
and Indian maid.
Only I knew
where the most
fragrant
mayflowers grew.

I paddled the early
dawn riverway
to the lilies
of my field;
to waxen green leaves
and shining white blooms,
and the knowing,
that if I wished,
I could walk
across them
to the shore.
Then out of youthful
need to disprove
childish belief
and knowing,
I would glide in
and watch them part
before my wood.

They were my stars
that I could touch,
that I could count,
as I tore root
from river bottom.

The soul should expand
in space of open
river and sky.
Remembering,
that night,
I wondered how
I did that;
I wondered why.

At the Hospital

While doctors told me
my father was a man
brain-stem-struck,
my inner eye sketched
broken-stalked
water lilies.

I never knew
there were deaths
such as this:
Locked in skull,
the brain
will turn,
and churn,
and strain,
and it is stuck.
They said that
with some luck
the heart muscle
stops as well.
Not so, with Father;
he was locked in Hell.

He had
no legs
to walk,
no hands
to touch,
no tongue
to speak.

He had only
rolling eyes,
searching,
searching,
voicing
questions,
spinning,
spinning,
within.

And one
dreadful,
pulsing-red
muscle,
beating
beating.
How long?
No one knew . . .
The body was
oak-strong

I asked if he was sane,
and listened to
prideful physicians explain
that they communicated
into his nothingess:
Two eye-blinks was "no"
and one was "yes."
I said,
"Nonsense. Why waste
those years we rode
the waterways with
Morse Code."

I crept into ICU
and instantly became
the little girl
he never knew,
when I said,
"Daddy, it's Red."

I heard him scream.
My solar center
felt the floor.
I had heard
screams before,
out of same dim
primal depths.
This was not him.

(I saw him mend
shipboard-cut,
teeth clenched,
whipping needle
through his skin.)
Could the pain
of seeing me
have wrenched
this cry?

Dread thoughts begin,
Dear God,
let him die.

I brought him
my mouthings;
whirlpool-words
sentence-spilled
from his prison
to my pen
and page.

I asked what
he would have
me do and
held my breath;
he dot and dashed,
"Give me Death."

We all have an early
appointment with Death
in some dark meeting place.
He has come beckoning
to us in dreams;
we know his shining face.

We all have an early
engagement with Death,
on some dimly-lit street,
for our names are entered
in his ledger and that
is one debt we must meet.

Anyone may call an early
rendezvous with Death,
but he must understand,
the Hooded Stranger may
not come his way,
may not accept his
proffered hand.

The black Angus bull
visited that first night.
He stood in the corral
of my dreams
rending the seams
of my reality.
It took five more
cartridges to bring
him, kneeling,
to the ground.

As I placed each
one in the rifle,
my feeling of
committing some
alien, sexual act
could not erase
the fact
he was refusing
to die on command.

Some swear oaths
by omens.
My Scottish family
seeress
would never scoff
at the potence of
that black beast's
hard dying the
week before.
The Infinite
prepares us
and we refuse to make
the connections,
preferring to toss
away His inward
suggestions
of the dire directions
our lives may take.

The next day,
I saw my pain
in his dark eyes,
then felt my pain
intensified;
I reached across
the void of space,
to take his hand,
to interface.

Our recent years had
not been our best.
Now, we needed the
touching for me
to guide him to
his long-last rest.

I laid my head
upon his pillow,
hand upon his brow,
and said,
"Father, you never
understood nor knew
the forces that
shaped me were
so unlike the
energy that
shaped you.
You bone-worked me
to fight my gut-grieve.
Now you must brain-work
to accept and believe.
You taught me to live.
My friend taught
me how to die.
We will reverse life's
river to its beginnings;
together just as before
you and I.

With lightning-struck clarity
and a pure presentiment,
I saw the certainty
that my dead Shaman-friend
had been God-sent.

There are some lives
that will not breathe
between constricting
lines of poetry.

He was a dark-skinned priest,
a dreamer of dreams,
life-spanning
one hundred plus-years
of dark history.

He called me Star Seeker
and more than that,
he called me daughter.
Jim never saw me,
not the physical me;
just my spirit.
I was honored to be
called daughter.

"Why waste energy
paddling your canoe
on a dry river bed?"

I had earned seven
letters, impotent
proclamations,
behind my name.
They did not
say who I was.
Jim was illiterate.
He knew.

"Sit quietly beside
the stream.
The Spirit will
bring you all
you need.
But first, you
must learn to see."

I became centered
in earth,
aware of continuous,
renewing flow of life,
and finally,
I saw the wind.

Jim was not cradled
by my world.
No lines of mine
could hold him now.

Father agreed
he had a need
to explore
new thought-paths;
we travelled
together with only
Jim's light to
guide the way
through the
backward forest
of Father's memory.

First, I had to pay
the price of his
patience-purchased
strength in me.
I pumped the iron of
the white-starched
institution
and their death-denying
of a man's dignity.

(There must be
restitution
somewhere for
bedeviling
the dying.)

I filled his need
to speak and
life-extenders sought
implicating motives
as I fought
for his right
to secede
in peace.

We did not hold in awe
new machines and old law
they worshipped.
They could not balance
weight of love he gave;
could not halt our
journey to his grave.

Alan Cameron
had a ten-day
walk beside
the river,
looking for
his boat across.
I walked the
same way.
We melded
our metals,
becoming alloyed
as we burned
and destroyed
the threads
tying him
to this plain.

Toward the last,
there was a surcease
of struggle;
He was approaching
the place of final peace.
When he stepped
aboard his ship,
I felt the inner
strand clip.
Numb, I watched
a sunbeam dance
in a graceful
melody of light
before the
sky moved and
it was night.

FATHER

What can I say of him . . .
The man who ran beside the bike;
Only that he was never like
Fathers that others had.

What can I tell of him . . .
The man with his hand on the seat
As he ran up and down the street.
That he knew how to love?

This I can say of him . . .
He always knew when to let go;
He taught me to balance just so,
Then let me ride alone.

L'CHAIM
(A Poet's History)

(2020)

TABLE OF CONTENTS

1940s
    Euterpe's Servant
    My Mother's Garden
    Father
    Zer'a

1950s
    Discovering Phillis Wheatley
    Abelard Speaks
    A Fifties Woman
    Tennessee Woman
    Gregory Ain
    Mid-Century Architect
    Always It Is One-on-One
    Weekend Hippies

1960s
    The Watts Towers
    Five Mile Radius
    Lori
    The Blooming

1970s
- Mourning The Diarist
- Critique
- Conversation
- On This Day
- Nebraska Talkin'
- The Muse of Lion Street
- The Quilter

1980s
- Walls
- Notes On Grenada
- The Texan
- Passing On The Sacred Task
- The Carolers
- My God
- The Haunting
- Chocolate Chip Date Cake

1990s
- My Friend Charles
- Reincarnation
- The Longhorn
- Final Gifts
- Infinity
- The Burden

2000s
- Chicago
- Lynne
- The Caledonian
- God's Critters Gotta Eat Somethin'
- The Couple
- Confirmation
- Hands
- The Convert
- Glued
- God's Bounty
- Retired

2010s
- Alchemy
- Profit and Loss Statement
- Au 'Voir
- Tides
- Jerusalem
- Dream Child
- Navi
- Anticipation
- The 45th President's Pride

2020s
- Ari's Song
- Note to Norrie
- Epitaph

1940s

Euterpe's Servant

When I
was young
my
loneliness
was wrapped
in a comforter
of words,
a cloisonne
quilt
of mosaic
meaning

I was
warm-loved.
by Barrett
and Browning;
I walked
on hills of
Wordworth's
daffodils,
and steamed
to school
aboard
Bliss Carmen's
Ships of Yule.

When grown,
I would
explain
I was
Euterpe's
servant
because,
in youth,
I was
word-slain.

My Mother's Garden

Who walks
in my
mother's garden
on such
a day
as this
when Spring's
wet wind
has descended
to give
Earth a
fierce kiss?
When each
slumbering
vine is
held in her
'passioned
embrace
and none
dare intrude
here save
one who
walks in
stately grace.

Who walks
where irises
lie sleeping
and ladies of
the valley hide?
Beauty wrapped
in Earth's keeping;
life watered
by the tears
we cried.
What Shade
walks in my
mother's garden
when night
is very still?
Mother's homey,
loving spirit
and strong,
abiding will.

Father

The Mira's
waters
were cold.
I was told
to swim.
I swam.
The boat
was docked
He cut
the rope.
I stopped
playing
and learned
to navigate.
(He also
taught
me things
I later
learned.
to hate.)

He spoke
of the
intricacies
of God
as he
challenged
youthful
disbelief,
guiding
my fingers
over the
dark green
ridges of
a leaf.

He taught me
to question
and to risk
the strife.
He taught me
to live life.

Zer'a

First came
chaos;
firmament,
then a
seed;
not an animal,
not man,
not woman,
(those non-survivors).

Thank God
for his
third day.

1950s

Discovering Phillis Wheatley
(c. 1753-1784)

She was
an ebony,
velvet orchid
growing in a
Boston
primrose
garden,
far from
jungle or
sordid
slavery block
of sad
southern
bargain.

She was a
favorite
sable pet,
an oddity
nurtured
by white
bonemeal,
lauding
white
freedom,

denouncing
pagan god
and black
soulseal.

Then John's
love taught
her to
breathe with
her own kind
as she wrote
ebony gems
from her
ebony mind.

She was
thrice
oppressed:
Talented woman,
black,
and slave;
subtle ripple,
first flow,
promising
future
tidal wave.

Abelard Speaks

They say you walk stately austere
And stern in Paraclete's garden,
Fingers wrapped in rosary prayer,
Lips curved in eternal pardon.

Our time was ensconced in dark night
When I was cruelly cut from heart,
Erasing bodies of delight
And voyages we would not chart.

Last night I dreamed we ran in fields,
You laughing, golden, skirts held high;
Then I woke to meager yields
Here, under St. Marcel's bleak sky.

My weighted heart is sickle-shorn;
You are my pain personified,
I am Prometheus re-torn
With male identity denied.

Your written words are beggar's alm
For begging soul that now implores;
For me there is no mercy's balm
Until my dead bones are bed with yours.

A Fifties Woman

She manipulates.
Never participates
in argument.
Never negotiates:
No solution.
No resolution.
She wins.

Her smile
is sweet.
Still,
she remains
incomplete
as she pays
the price of
powerless
survival.

Tennessee Woman

I knew a Tennessee woman;
She was an autoharp queen.
Never knew where she was going,
But knew, for sure, where she'd been.

She had picked all her golden flowers,
Petals then scattered away,
Knowing the time for picking flowers
In bright grass on sunlit day.

She'd drunk the waters of her well,
Tasting bitterness and pain;
Found her water sweet just then,
And all that could change again.

She'd looked through windows of discord,
They were everywhere, she found;
So she nurtured her serenity
In mind and autoharp sound.

I knew a Tennessee woman
And she lives within this song:
Lone, not lonely, and always one
With the road she walked along.

Gregory Ain
Mid-Century Architect

We met where
and when
neither
should have
been.

We had
forgotten our
eons past
and that
our now
could never
last.

Your shadow
reached
for mine;
we touched
but those
shadows
never did
entwine.

I was
red-headed
brash,

vibrating
in the
bright
while you
were
white-haired
shy and
lived in
dappled
light.

You were
never a
climber, Greg.
You were
Wright's
student
with your
own plan,
so tiptoed
into your
own
fame-pool
by building
homes for
the common
man.

It was
McCarthy's
time
(blessedly brief)
but you were
caught in that
yellow-stained
web of grief.
Thumbscrew
torture
was wielded
when your
mind-skills
were denied.
Sometimes,
Politics can
be evil but,
eventually,
evil will be
decried.

Daily, Greg,
I drive by
houses of your
mid-century
design.
I smile,
knowing you
live on in
praises
of your style.

Always It Is One-on-One

A Gentile
held the
chuppah
when
she was
married
in Berlin.
Life was fragile
then and
four of
family
could not
be found.

(The Gentile
was buried
with a
hundred
others in
unconsecrated
ground.)

She lived
and lost
through
Holocaust
to eat
Pesach's
bitter herbs
of freedom.
But always,
when the
curious asked
where was
the hate
she carried,
she smiled
and said,
"A Gentile
held my
chuppah when
I was married."

Weekend Hippies

Hello, Big Daddy,
Come sing us a song:
Your mouth is
three yards wide,
Your toga,
Six yards long.

It was
a time for
Joan Baez,
flowery skirts,
long, red hair
clinging to
my back,
and we were
blowing in
the wind.

Friday nights
we met at
Big Daddy's
Venice
storefront
where the
oracle
would flaunt
his massive
bedsheet-
clad self.

He would
tell us how
to be free;
I read
Ginsburg's
poetry,
and Ralph
beat his
bongo drum.

Saturday:
We sought
cigarette
money
under sofa
cushions
and Don
came by
with the
funny pills
I was not
brave enough
to try.
We were still
blowing in
the wind
while Ralph
beat his
bongo drum.

Sunday we
returned to
ritual,
leaving
Big Daddy
and his
meringue
content.
I shopped,
then ironed
my office
uniform
and never
questioned
where
Big Daddy
went.
Ralph
put down
his drum
and his
cool
in favor
of his
sliderule.
And, we
were
still
blowing
in the wind.

1960s

The Watts Towers

Last night the
communicating
Cyclops
handed me
Sam's head
while a
disembodied
voice said
he was a
Great American
and there
was a series
of them.

A series of Sam?
No way!
I laughed
and spiraled
back to that
1960's day
when
I first stood
in that sad
neighborhood
staring at
Sam Rodia's
towers.

I was pierced
forever by the
creator's powers.

Thirty years
that lonely
man
grubbed and
garnered the
railroad track
that clung
to the Angel City's
underbelly and
grey ghetto's
back.

He sought
glimmer
and glit,
(our discarded
skin scales)
and fit
us into his
transcendent
backyard frames
of ascendant
mud and steel.

I was young;
fire seeking
a cause
when
bureaucratic
city claws
tore at
Sam's spires.
We fought
and lost to
City Laws.
Italy's shy,
illiterate gift
ran before
the onslaught.

We won.
The Law
could not
press him
into dust.
The air
cleared and
three fingers
indexed
Heaven's line:
God's Plan,
Sam's Design.

Five Mile Radius

Hickory-rigid,
her spine
flexed in
retirement
time as she
tended
morning glories
by her door;
she lived,
peering with
magnified eyes
through
children's eyes,
sitting surrounded
on nursery floor.

Forty years
she taught,
while time
advanced
from country
crowded,
single room
to modern
concrete school;

and always
she followed
students from
primer page to
marriage lines,
all of them
gifted to
swim in her
knowledge
pool.

Now she
talked with
dolls and
Teddy bears
and drank
imaginary tea.
My little ones
went to bed,
dreaming
geranium dreams
she planted in
each head.
And then,
she made my
kitchen warm,
paring apples
with me.

At day's rest
I watched her
stride across
my meadow,
antiquated
poke bonnet
shading brow,
sturdy legs
owning land
I owned
in the
temporary now.

She was
a living,
five mile
radius of
Nebraska's
story
who
introduced
me to the
five mile
radius of me.

Lori

Renoir's
girl with
the golden
hair
stood beside
my bed
offering air
in her
open hand.
I did not
Understand
so when
she was
only three
I ate her
Imaginary
bunny.

When she
was five
we talked
of fairy trees
and other
mysteries;
we found
a giraffe
hiding
behind a
dryad,
assuming

the shape
of an oak,
and then
we spoke
of what
was true:
that grass
is not green
and the sky
is not blue,
my full
of wonder
child.

She is my
gentle child,
my never
wild child,
the need
to ponder
child.

Whoever
she is
meant
to be,
her life
poetry
will
utilize
the best
of me.

The Blooming

I built
a house
upon a
hill
where
burning bush
and
Joseph's coat
spill;
life was
a surfeit
yet I
yearned
for more;
Now I tend
one rose
on a desert
floor.

The unique,
unexpected
rose
blooms and
pierces,
I suppose,
to her own
rhythms,
in her own
seasons;
there is
no way
I may close
errant
heart-shutters
to the throes
of her
embedded thorn,
of her
embedded joy.

1970s

Mourning The Diarist

His strong script
disappears
around
the edge
of my
life's page.
Remembrance
births
more tears
as grief
marries
loss and rage.

I continue
to read his
leather-bound
years.

This
hotel room
imprisons
my emotion.
No fierce
ocean
of pain
will be
sorrow-
impressed
on the

home walls
of our nest.

This is my last
indulgence of
cherishing
time
with him;
a time
to share
his secret
diarist's whim.

I read slowly,
reluctant
to approach
the end,
his final words
stealing
my own
breath.

But now
I must
snip his
life's last
thread
and send
this
private part
of him
to death.

Critique

You
are the
McDonald's
of poetry,
she said,
while I am
haute
cuisine.

I asked,
What does
that mean?
Words
cheaply
bought?
More
calories
per thought?

I was
always
a scribbler,
bereft of
Ginny's
fine poet's
palate.
Johnson's
Boswell
would have
called me
poetaster,
but never
a petty poet.

Conversation

Sure, Friend,
We walked
for equality
and I was
there,
but I was
contrarily
apart.

I was cloaked
in historic
reference
and impatient
over cruel
deference.
I marched
to honor
your tribal
story,
your
right to
not be me.

We are not
the same,
Friend.
But that
does not
make you
devil-dark
and me
angel-light.

We both
deserve
like-liberty.
Still, we are
not the same.

You remain
my beginnings;
I remain your
shattered
history.

On This Day

Rosenthal,
the L. A.
journalist,
wrote,
"The world
waited as
Armstrong
dressed
to go out."

"He is
one of us,"
the minister
said.
So Aldrin
carried
consecrated
bread.

Collins
waited,
unfettered,
yet wearing
our chains;
always alone
within our
earth-bound
brains.

The L. A.
wino said,
"Those guys
got grit",
and his voice
had rare
remembrance
in it.

Nebraska Talkin'

Elmer's cuttin',
but that milo
of mine needs
rain bad,
and it ain't
as though
he never had
a good crop
last year.

Do Your Will,
Ya hear.
All I can
ask for me
is no
catastrophe.

Roger's fightin',
like as not
some other
farmer's son;
there's nothin'
special he's
ever done
'cept work
this here land.

Hold him in
Your Hand.
Hold that
other boy too.
I s'pose he
talks to You.

I'm 'tasslin'
and it
helps to talk
things over
now and then;
this year's.
wheat tested
at eleven.
Hard winter,
fair year,
Do Your Will,
Ya hear.
All I can
ask for me
is no
catastrophe.

The Muse of Lion Street

I left her
behind
in Alabama
and she sat
on the
backburner
of my mind,
unwilling
to be
pressed
between
my lines.

We met
over sprouts
in the
health food
store
and soon
shared
history over
chamomile tea.
She called
herself
Africa

and Africa
she was, a
Victoria Falls
of creativity.

Her fingers
caressed
Chopin;
her voice
soared,
chocolate rich
sublime;
she stretched
her walls
with
self-made
rugs of
primitive
design,
while I
developed
a taste
for the
savory paste
of her
metaphors.

I asked why
she left
Mozart, and
even Ellington,
and saw
the color
of her rage;
"How many
Blacks have
you seen
on the
concert stage?"

After that
I tread her
shallows
afraid I
might drown
in her deep.

I left her
in Alabama
before she
moved along
to write her
Texas song.
Now I
listen for
Africa's
drumbeat
vibrating
through
Houston's
Lion Street.

The Quilter

HaShem,
quilt me
with
brilliant
patches:
squares of
yesterday.

Sew me
days
well lived,
 worked in
denim and
calico.
Blend
dark green
velvet-grief
with child-joy
crimson.

HaShem,
thread me
with
tenderness
to cover,
to shelter
family.

Quilt me
with love,
HaShem.

1980s

Walls

His was
opaque,
not brick
baked
but well
engineered,
perhaps
teflon or
titanium
based.

It was a
masterpiece,
that wall;
too high
to climb,
too deep to
penetrate.
He curled
behind it,
unable to
communicate.

Her construct was a fifties cubic design: hunky chunks of blue glass. She preened behind those prisms; blissful in Imprisonment, never to accomplish her own becoming.

Notes On Grenada

Raymond Darby:
"What do you do, Missus?"
Soft patois
plucks at
my sleeve.
"I believe I
write poetry".
"You have a book?"
Wire bracelets
frame
elegant hands
that squeeze
my heart and
hypnotize.
I nod yes,
looking down
on mocha face
into licorice eyes.

"You bring your book
and I sell it here."
Shirt and trousers
starch-pressed,
I resist
joy-seizing him
to my breast.
I know I must
not crush a
twelve year old
entrepreneur.

Asher McLeod:
"I am an Israelite."
White teeth
flash in black
beneath a
wool-drenched cap.
My daughter,
wearing the Star
over her heart
and within,
says,
"I am a Levite."

They grip hands
and grin.
He sits,
working ropes,
telling of
his hopes
for the
cargo race.
Standing on
his boat
I wonder
how these
rotting boards
will stay afloat
until tomorrow.

Captain Windy:
"Lost the leg
at twenty-one;
a conch
coral cut
while diving;
gangrene,
and it was
done."
My skin
Shrivels from
water-soaked sun.
"Been more
places
on one leg
than ever
could on two."
He treats me
to a gaping smile
but his
milk-stained,
dark eyes
whisper
pain.
I wait for
him to speak
again.

"Never thought
I would see
a man die
hard or
disappear
'til Cubans
herded friends
and brothers
through the
streets
this year."

As I step
on land;
he takes
my hand.
"Missus, you
 tell them,
G-d bless
your President
and the troops
he sent."

The Texan

He was a
Melville
mountain
eagle
flying
far above
our plain.

He was a
T-Rex
businessman
waving
yellow-stained
fingers,
boasting
with
teenage
fervor of
how he
beat
the big
"C".
(Just like
John Wayne.)

He was a
rough,
bluff,
arrogant,
self-made
man.

And I still
listen
for his
cowboy boots
on the
stairs,
stomping
that
long ago
painful path.

He was an
acquiring
man,
always
working,
always
needing:
The mansion,
the pool,
the wives.
the elaborate
golf clubs,
the Lamborghini.

They only
needed my
signature
to open
his grave.

Passing On The Sacred Task

Rosi came late.
Hungry,
after school,
she sat
in the
car and
ate.

Then
she smiled
at the
kippah-clad
guardian
at the
gate
and joined
her sisters
in prayer.

They prayed
for purity;
to be
cleansed
as they
cleansed;

they prayed
for holy
guidance to
faithfully
fulfill this
mitzvah.

They donned
aprons and
hands
that peeled
potatoes
warmed
cold flesh.
They spoke as
midwives do of
small chatty
things:

Of her
unlined brow
and the
beauty of
her bones;
how they
wished

they knew
her Hebrew
name
for the
other was
impotent
now.

Rosi washed
and dried
soft, white
hair while
voices
rippled in
harmony
to water
spraying
on lividity

She helped
lift her
sister for
dressing
in the
three piece
shroud,

trying not
to be too
proud
of her young
strength.

When
the hood
was wrapped
around
her head,
the cloth
placed upon
her face
they looked
the length
of their labor
and Miriam,
The elder,
said,

"We did our
best, Dear;
we hope
it was enough."

The Carolers

Four plus two
songbirds
met on a
Parkland Hospital
Dallas street:
First came
the nightingale,
then three
Broadway
bound;
all joined
by a glorious
basso profundo
and his friend
the red crow;
all intent on
making a
joyous sound,
wafting an AIDS
Christmas round.

They chose to
ignore the
vicious fear
confining

them to the
fringe;
they chose
to ignore that
T-cells could
disappear.
They sang
because they
shared a
nightmare that
none could
comprehend.
Within those
walls each
had a friend
dying of
an acronym.

Five of the
Christmas
songbirds
flew away
and lived on.
The next
year the
glorious
basso profundo
was gone.

My God

HaShem
is in the
Candles,
in the
Brachah,
in Aliyah.

Adonai
is in the
Torah
and in
holy
Silence.

Elohim
dwells
most of
all in the
Detritus of
Humanity.

The Haunting

Ours
is a
free
space of
random
rhyme,
far from
delicate
lace of
sonnet
time.

Why must
I write?
Because I
cannot
not.

Words
search
me out:
They haunt,
they taunt,
they
proliferate:
I cannot
escape
trudge
fleeing
fudge
or
anonymous
pursuing
cacophonous.

So why do
I write?
Because I
cannot
not.

Chocolate Chip Date Cake

The devil
came to
Danvers
(Salem
Village then).

Centuries
later he
visited my
husband's
mother,
residing
behind her
prideful
cookie jar
as she
spoke of
possession
by the
Demon of
Humility.
I did not
query
how that
could be.

I heard
a lie
self-sewn
into her
apron
far from
the pocket
where her
good sense
had flown.

The evil
I could see
was the
missing
ingredient
in her
every
shared
recipe.

1990s

My Friend Charles

He was an
eighties,
hair-styled,
boyish,
monogrammed
man.

He attempted
elegance,
achieved
education,
loved
students
too well.

Plague
ridden,
he died
of loving
too well.

He was
clever.
He was
caustic.
He would
have
hated
growing
old.

Reincarnation

That last
night
we sat,
fingers
entwined,

He asked.
I answered,
expressing
comfort
in my
economy
of souls
theory.

He smiled
and true
to his
Naturalist
calling,
he said
he would
like to
return as
a tree.

I smile now,
wondering.
Does he
stand beside
this
cool brook,
wind
ruffling
his leaves?

The Longhorn

In 1860
longhorns
grew on
Texas plains,
six to one of
humankind.

No longer
majestic,
he stood
in the
corral.
Tears
deep-tunneled
his cheeks.
Steve said
he was
lonely
and would
daily
stand,
wearily
weeping.

She understood.
Then wondered
when her
kind would
enter
that same
sad pool of
obsolescence.

Final Gifts

Words.
Hers were
written,
a sharing of
Virginia's
thoughts
and pride;
strong love
of family,
unproclaimed
alive.

His were
spoken after
fifty-three
years:
"I would
not change
a thing"
he told
Jean.
His eyes
closed,
his hand
slipped
from hers.

The finest
gifts
could be
words.

Infinity

I walk a
moebius
strip
toward
eternity
finding
there
much of
Thee,
much
of me.

I plant
a sapling
that grows
toward
eternity.
In that
tree is
much of
Thee,
much
of me.

I sing
my own
song of
love unto
eternity
to become
much of
Thee,
much of
me.
Thee,
me,
Thee,
Thee,
Thee…

The Burden

Yesterday,
my friend,
the Rabbi,
made the
cuckoo sing.

He worked
clock weights
and mused,
"Burdens
bring rewards."

Today,
my friend
the scholar,
received
his burden:
Alzheimers.

HaShem.
What
will be
his reward?

2000s

Chicago

The first
called it
Smelly Waters.

It is
raw youth,
noisome,
corrupted
talent.
It is
old Irish,
younger Slavs
struggling
Africans.
All burrito
wrapped
around selves,
shoving outward,
clawing upward.
All demanding
their share,
sweating
their deserves.

She fell on
Jackson St.
A cadavered,
dark-skinned
man,
perhaps
homeless,
rushed to
lift her to
the curb.

She sat there,
bleeding,
ignored.
Just she
and one
kind man.
An old city,
Smelly Waters,
with no welcome
for the old.

Lynne

I loved you:
Woman to woman,
heart to heart;
definitely apart
from any
physicality.

It was your hands.
I sat in your
workshop
and saw
them stroke
the leather.
I was in
such awe
of your
capability.

It was your
strong will.
You would
see some
new trail,
change
direction;
and without
fail,

you would
make it work.

It was your mind.
It was full
of rainbow
butterflies.
You chased them all
while I was
too wise
to follow.

Remember
that winter
you shared
my fairyland.
I cared
that you
would turn
to me
in pain.
We laughed
and saw
the world
through a less
distorted glass
and then
you were
gone again.

The Caledonian

You are
the thistle,
Kay,
great clots of
Scotland
clinging to
your roots.

You are
subtle as
skirling
pipes,
and fierce
as the
Ladies
from hell
who
haunted
the Hun.

Kay,
I am
dead cert
you
triumphed at
Bannockburn
and died at
Culloden;

that you
grew in
Jacobite
caves of
despair
and rose
again to
meet Shon.

The rose
will fade
beneath
bridal feet;
lads and lassies
will tear
petals
from the
marguerite.
But
the loyal
thistle
will
survive.
She will stand,
And stand
for Scotland.
Blessed Be,
Kay.

God's Critters Gotta Eat Somethin'

Today:
Toronto boy
found
maggots
in the garbage.
He writhed
with
scavengers
while flooding
the pail.

Today:
My lines
flew away,
aloft,
between
white barn
and wood;
spiraling
toward
Pearson's
Pond

I chased
liltings
to the
Parker River
where they
fed fish.

Today:
The fisherman
gave us surplus
trout.
Were we
scavengers?
Did we eat my words?

The Couple

Early each
morning
the old
couple
walk,
hand in
hand.

Late loving
has a sure
sweetness
to it,
devoid of
demands,
devoid of
youth's
frantic
passion.

Yesterday's lessons have been learned:
Late loving is not married to tomorrow.

Late loving has skills and wondrous knowing that neither is broken by the others going.

The loving was,
is,
and always…

Confirmation

I could
not go.

She went,
paid for
the tour;
paid to
accept
horror and
tzorris,
bone deep.

Returning,
she could
only say,
"the birds-
the birds;
they don't
sing there."

Birds
do not
sing at
Dachau.

I replied,
"Why
would
they?"

Hands

Many girls
in my youth
were not good
at sisterhood
or sharing truth.

Our more-imposed
restrictions
silenced
convictions
that elders
could bear
guilt or any sin.

Some women
opened
with age,
exposing
niblings,
cookie crumbs
of their
beginnings.

She spoke
of shameful
first love:
A businessman,
Warden of
her church,
family
friend.

And always,
She described
His hands:
Hands
expertly
spanning
The ivories;
hands
expertly
fondling
her nubility;
Hands
ruining her
for any
other man.

The Convert

Her anger
was paint
thrown
on the
wind,
touching
everywhere,
landing
nowhere.

Her journey
was arduous.
She was no
Dorothy
dancing a
yellow brick
road.
She plodded
through
Dante's
landscapes,
all nine rings;
knew hells
of yearning,
until she
turned to
battle
Amalek.

Until she
won,
becoming
the rock,
Moriah.
Then,
the Torah
rested in
her arms.

Glued

Labels
are easy
to attach;
they may
adhere
for a
lifetime.

The waters
were
fearfully
dark as
she crossed
the Sound.
She was
nauseous
from
circumstance,
not sea;
then made
sicker by
strangeness
in a strange city.

She paid
the bail,

then begged
a beggar to
lead her
to the jail.

At seventy-five
she struggled
against the
label of
martyr
affixed
by her
children.

And then,
as always,
she did
what she
had to do.

Labels:
Martyr?
Mother?

God's Bounty

How can
we show
charity
When our
lives are
Blessing
bound?

How can
there be
giving
when all
was gifted?

We have
debt and
any giving is
interest due,
never to be
completely
paid.

Retired

No regrets,
he said,
to pierce or
splinter
memory.

He has
relived
scenarios
of then;
they
provoke
the same
response.
If he
had been
wrong,
he would
be wrong
again.

Now,
there is
comfort in
familiarity:

His old
boat,
his full life,
Mementos,
and
grandchildren.

He has no
harbor for
regrets.
He has
retired
them.

2010s

Alchemy

We have
not the
alchemy
to turn
our present
base years
golden.

Some have
thin years,
tin years.
Others have
copper years,
the taste
of blood
in mouth.

Some have
years of
silver slivers
embedded
in wealth;
piercing years.

We lack
alchemy
yet we
have
elements:
Passion's
fire flares;
earth gives
flowered
fragrance;
birth waters
flow with
grandchildren
and
the air-
the air-
celebrates
with songs
of past
and present joy.

We may
lack
alchemy
but who
can say
these years
HaShem
has given
are not
golden?

Profit and Loss Statement

She clings
to her
debits:
Husband,
tennis,
driving.

She ignores
her assets:
Children,
abundant friends,
and her
Puget Sound
view.

Sadly,
she has
lost the
lush
memory
of love
shared
where
azaleas
grew.

Au 'Voir

How do
I say
goodbye
to a
long-ago
lover
when
lustful
tides
have
ebbed
with age?

Loving days
now
reside in
comfort's
arms and
friendship's
bed.

Still,
I see that
Renaissance
Man
in his
old white
truck;
I fly in his
small plane
over

bluebells
and Indian
paint brush.
We walk
in high
Colorado
meadows,
and lie
together in
dark Texas
corners.

Once,
I said,
"I must
go first.
This heart
will not
abide a
lonely
void."

He was
first to
sleep.
Now
I mourn
but I am
treasure-
filled
and
will not
weep.

Tides

Martyr.
(Scorn).
Crushed flower.
(Anger).

Scab-scraped
daughter
words;
acid dripped
on old,
still open
sores;

Wounding
words,
bracketing
stores of
kindness.
(She left
the
cruelest
unsaid.)

Later,
the tide was
coming in.
We walked
the beach,
two women
striding
together
With mutual
rhythm.

We spoke of
Rod Serling's
Twilight Zone,
lost highways,
and hidden
history,
scouring bone.

The tide was
coming in.

Jerusalem

It is
uphill to
Jerusalem:
From the
airport,
from the
Dead Sea.

I have
flown
in joy;
I have
sunk
in dark
waters.

Never,
never
have I
followed
the
pink-stoned
path to
Jerusalem;
never
known
Lyn's
ecstasy.

It is
uphill to
Jerusalem.

Dream Child

The waves
slap the
dock on
Stone
Valley
Lake
and I
remember
misty Mira
mornings
and begin
to weave
the wake
of the child
who never
became.

We all
own a ten
year old
of varied
shining themes
sitting
at the
edge of
our dreams:

The child
who
seldom
becomes.

I am
eighty
this
Mother's Day
at Stone
Valley
Lake.
I stand
while
waters
lick the
salt toes
of the first
of my
unrealized
rainbows.
And I let go.

Navi

Prophets:
Joseph,
Ezekiel,
Jeremiah,
Daniel.

To be,
to see
beyond.
To know
The Presence:

To be.
I accept
Navi.

Anticipation

A headache
becomes a
precursor
of a stroke;
a twinge
in the chest,
a heart
attack;
a thickness
in the
breast,
cancer.

Such are
the small
terrors
of aging.

In youth,
we did
not know
we could
die.

But now?
Listen!
The deaf
can feel
it as well:
The
ominous
music
the killer
hides
behind
before
lunging
in the
horror
flick.

Remember
when we
thrilled
to that
tempo?

It is
still an
ending
option.

The 45th President's Pride

Plastic flags and wet girls on parade,
All of them stamped "American Made."

All of them wave as they go by,
Art only nature dares defy.

Wet flags and plastic girls on parade,
See the girls break, oh see the flags fade.

2020s

Ari's Song

I will
love you,
perhaps
not the
way you
want
me to
love you.
And,
I will
love you.

When I
am gone
you will
glimpse
me but
I will be
fleet.
You will
hear me
whisper
the Shema
as you
drift into
sleep

and
you will
feel my
hand on
your cheek
if you
have
occasion
to weep.

I know
your time
and
I know
your space,
a thousand
years your
changing
face;
a thousand
years your
onward pace.

And
I will
love you.

Note to Norrie

You are gone,
Toronto Boy.
Was it easier
to just leave?

I guess you
stopped
looking-
looking,
for you.

You wrapped
religions
around you
but none
melded with
your spirit.

You tinkered
with occupations;
none fit.

You did
good deeds
but you
did not
value them
yourself.

Your carnal love
did not work
because you
could not
love you.

I am so sorry,
Toronto Boy,
because there
was something
in you I
sort of liked.

Epitaph

I hope
when they
put me
in the
ground
a few of
my friends
will stand
around
and say,
"Her
last lines
were not
her best";
and,
"She was
ready for
her long
rest."

Please let
one say,
"She bore
witness but
sharing laughter
was more
her way."

I pray
they will
know
my life
was a
love and joy
filled cup
and I drank
to the dregs
until I was
all used up.

ACKNOWLEDGMENT

I would like to express my appreciation of Nancy Chiswick, who has worked tirelessly to bring this book to fruition. It would never have happened without her, nor would it without the support of Penny Eifrig. There is nothing stronger than women supporting women.

M.D.C.

www.ingramcontent.com/pod-product-compliance
Lightning Source LLC
Chambersburg PA
CBHW060519080526
44586CB00012B/543